Contents

LIVEWIRE
INVESTIGATES

The Black Death

Pu

Hodder & Stoughton

Acknowledgements

Cover: Dave Smith

Illustrations: Sally Michel

Every effort has been made to trace copyright holders of material reproduced in this book. Any rights not acknowledged will be acknowledged in subsequent printings if notice is given to the publisher.

Orders; please contact Bookpoint Ltd, 39 Milton Park, Abingdon, Oxon OX14 4TD. Telephone: (44) 01235 400414, Fax: (44) 01235 400454. Lines are open from 9.00–6.00, Monday to Saturday, with a 24 hour message answering service.
Email address: orders@bookpoint.co.uk

British Library Cataloguing in Publication Data
A catalogue record for this title is available from the British Library

ISBN 0 340 77644 7

First published 2000
Impression number   10 9 8 7 6 5 4 3 2 1
Year   2005 2004 2003 2002 2001 2000

Copyright © 1999 NTC/Contemporary Publishing Group, Inc.

Adapted for the Livewire series by Sarah Blackmore

Typeset by GreenGate Publishing Services, Tonbridge, Kent.
Printed in Great Britain for Hodder and Stoughton Educational, a division of Hodder Headline Plc, 338 Euston Road, London NW1 3BH, by Redwood Books, Trowbridge, Wilts

1 Bring Out Your Dead!

Bring out your dead!
Bring out your dead!

That was the cry.
It could be heard all over Europe
in the 1300s.
The cry of the cart drivers.
Driving the carts pulled by horses.
Carts filled with dead bodies.

Bodies were dragged from almost every house.
Dragged out and thrown onto the carts.
Body was tossed on top of body.
Piles of dead bodies.
Like logs in a pile of wood.

Sometimes two or three bodies
would be dragged from the same house.
The Black Death had struck.
The plague!

The Black Death killed people.
It killed lots of people.

In a large Russian city only five people lived
after the plague.
In London, nine out of every ten people
died of the plague.
In some other countries almost everybody died.

Can you imagine so many dead people?
It was not long before there were
no coffins left.
Dead bodies were thrown on top of each other.
They were piled high in huge pits.
Then a thin layer of dirt was thrown over them.

2 No Escape

The plague spread very quickly.
It spread from person to person.
People went to bed well.
The next day they were dead.

A doctor might try to treat somebody
with the plague.
Then the doctor would catch it as well.
The doctor died with the patient.
Sometimes even before.

Some doctors tried to protect themselves.
They wore a type of mask.
It looked like a large beak.
The beak was filled with things
that had a strong smell –
things like vinegar or sweet oils.
This stopped the doctors from smelling
dead or dying people.

They even used a rod
to take the patient's temperature.
They did not want to touch them.

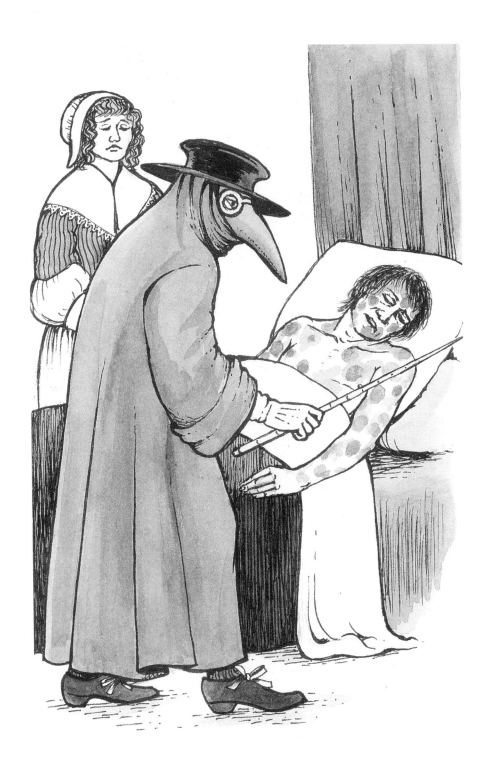

People tried to get away from the plague.
They tried to get away from each other.
Husbands left wives.
Parents left children.
Many people tried to leave the towns
and cities.
They thought that they would be safe
in the country.
They were wrong.
There was no escape from the plague.

3 Why the 'Black' Death?

The plague meant death,
but why was it called the 'Black' Death?

Let's imagine that you have the plague.
First you find lumps.
There may be lumps under your arms
or in your groin.
Lumps the size of eggs.
You will have a bad cough.
A really bad cough.
You will sweat a lot.
Added to this you will have black patches
all over your skin.
You will be dead in three days.

Ring a ring of roses
A pocket full of posies
Atishoo! Atishoo!
We all fall down.

This children's song is about the plague.

Ring a ring o'roses
The first sign of the plague was lumps.
They were spots or blisters
with rings round them.
They were rose coloured.

A pocket full of posies
Some people carried a posy of flowers
in their pocket.
They thought it would protect them.
It also helped to get rid of the smell
of people dying.

Atishoo! Atishoo!
One of the last symptoms of the plague
was sneezing.

We all fall down
After sneezing, people died.

4 How did it Spread?

So where did the plague come from?
Where did it start?

It started in China.
It spread very quickly
through lots of countries.
It came to Great Britain in 1348.

How did the plague spread?
We know that it spread
from person to person.
When people moved from one country to another
they took it with them.

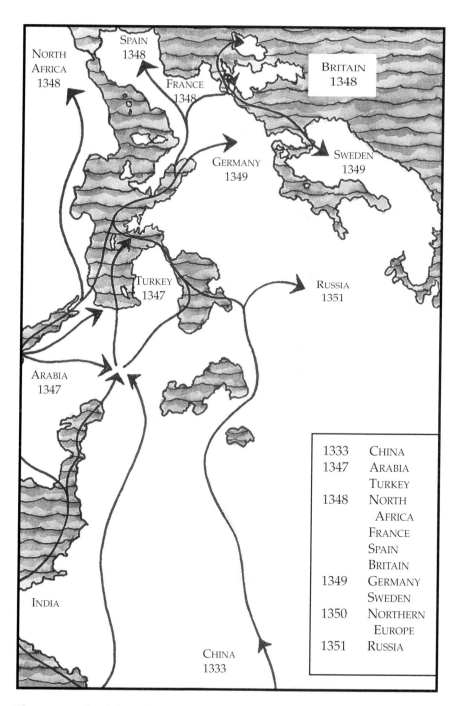

NORTH
AFRICA
1348

SPAIN
1348

FRANCE
1348

BRITAIN
1348

GERMANY
1349

SWEDEN
1349

TURKEY
1347

RUSSIA
1351

ARABIA
1347

INDIA

CHINA
1333

1333	CHINA
1347	ARABIA
	TURKEY
1348	NORTH AFRICA
	FRANCE
	SPAIN
	BRITAIN
1349	GERMANY
	SWEDEN
1350	NORTHERN EUROPE
1351	RUSSIA

The spread of the plague.

An army of people called the Tartars
fought across Europe.
They took the plague with them.
One story tells of how the Tartars
used dead bodies.
Bodies of those who had died of the plague.

They used huge catapults
to throw stones against walls.
They did this to fight their way
into towns and cities.
At one city the Tartars did not use stones.
They loaded the catapults with dead bodies.
They threw the bodies over the city walls.

Just think how quickly the plague spread.
Some of the people in the city ran away.
They took the plague with them.

The Black Death spread so quickly.
It killed so many people,
in so many countries.
Many people thought that it was the end
of the world.

5 An Act of God

Some people thought that the plague
had been sent by God.
They thought that God must be
very angry with them.
People who thought this
got together in groups.
They tried to punish themselves
for making God angry.
They dressed in sackcloth and ashes.
They beat themselves with whips
made of leather.
The whips had metal tips on the end.
By doing this they hoped that God
would stop the Black Death.

People were so scared of the plague.
It made them think and do all sorts of things.
Nobody knew how the plague had started.
Nobody knew if there was a cure.

As time went on, food began to run out.
The people who farmed the land
were all dying.
There was no one left to tend the crops.
Fields were full of dead animals.

When would it end?

6 The Cause

What did cause the plague?
There were lots of ideas.

One idea was that there were cracks
in the Earth.
People thought that the cracks were caused
by planets passing too close to Earth.
They thought that gas was coming out
of the cracks.
The gas was poison.
It caused the plague.

Do you believe that?

People did not know what had caused
the plague.
Because they did not know the cause,
they could not work out a cure.
They did all sorts of crazy things.

They tried anything to get rid of
the Black Death.
Some ate lizards and toads.
Some drank blood and other disgusting things.
Some ripped open the bodies of puppies
and birds.
They held them against the boils on their bodies.

Was there a cure?
What could it be?

What did cause the Black Death?
Something had to carry the plague germs.
Something did.
Rats!

Well, the fleas on rats.
The plague germ was in the fleas.
The fleas lived on the rats.
They drank their blood.

The fleas then jumped onto people.
Flea bites spread the plague in humans.

7 An End to the Plague

The plague went on and on.
This Black Death lasted for about 200 years.
Then it died away.

Some people think that the plague was
stopped by fire.
The Fire of London in 1666.
This great fire killed most of the rats
and the fleas with them.

So was fire the answer?
Was that the cure for the plague?
No.

For 200 years the Black Death killed people.
It spread all over Europe.
It was caused by flea bites
but could be passed from person to person.
A disease that can be passed on in this way
is called contagious.

If only people had known more about germs
back in 1300.
Today we know how important it is
to keep things clean.
Think about how clean our hospitals are.
Keeping things clean
protects us from some germs.
Soap and water could have helped
to protect people from the Black Death.
If only they'd known …

NOW WASH YOUR HANDS!